COMMONSENSE VEGETARIANISM

Written with the new convert and the interested non-vegetarian in mind, this book states clearly the facts and fictions of vegetarianism, and puts forward suggestions for the planning of a well-balanced, wholesomely appetizing and health-promoting vegetarian diet.

By the same author
BETTER SIGHT WITHOUT GLASSES
EVERYBODY'S GUIDE TO NATURE CURE
YOUR DIET IN HEALTH AND DISEASE

COMMONSENSE VEGETARIANISM

by

HARRY BENJAMIN N.D.

THORSONS PUBLISHERS LIMITED
Wellingborough, Northamptonshire

First published 1950
Second Impression 1955
Third Impression 1963
Fourth Impression 1967
Fifth Impression 1970
Sixth Impression 1972
Second Edition (completely revised and reset) 1974
Second Impression 1975
Third Impression 1977

ISBN 0 7225 0243 5

Typeset in Great Britain by
Specialised Offset Services Ltd, Liverpool
and printed by
Weatherby Woolnough Ltd., Sanders Road
Wellingborough, Northampton

CONTENTS

PREFACE TO FIRST EDITION

It has seemed to the author for some time now that a book on vegetarianism is desirable. The subject is one that has already received considerable attention in the past, but nothing has yet been done to attempt to bring its presentation into line with modern thought and ideas, and the latest scientific findings on diet and nutrition. It is this lack which the present book sets out to rectify, and it is sincerely hoped it will prove of value to many who wish to take up vegetarianism and thereby improve their health.

There cannot be the slightest doubt that a sensibly prepared meatless diet directly contributes towards improved health and fitness of mind and body, although a badly arranged and thoughtlessly prepared vegetarian dietary can lead to directly opposite results, as many vegetarians have found to their cost.

It is indeed this aspect of the matter to which I wish to devote most attention in this book, as the need for expert guidance in arranging a meatless dietary is all-important, otherwise the vegetarian may find himself the victim of all kinds of physical disabilities.

People who adopt vegetarianism from the purely ethical point of view, *i.e.* because they object to taking life, are the most prone to error here. They assume that because they are obeying what they deem to be a 'higher law' that law will automatically protect them from making mistakes and coming to any harm in their choice of a vegetarian diet. Nothing could be farther from the truth. Those who adopt vegetarianism, whether from ethical or purely health principles, are equally in need of guidance in the matter of choice and selection of food, and it is hoped this book will provide the necessary assistance.

At the same time, in view of current misconceptions about vegetarianism and vegetarian principles, it is as well to go over the ground fully and meet all possible objections and difficulties. With that idea in mind this book starts with a review of the whole subject, in which criticism of vegetarians themselves (and some of the erroneous views they themselves often hold) is also included.

It is felt that this is a most necessary pre-requisite to the full development of the subject, because many vegetarians tend to deter other people from becoming vegetarians because of their manner of conduct, and also because of some of the silly ideas they hold (and are always putting forward to non-vegetarians).

The author has been a strict vegetarian since 1926, with nothing but benefit to health and well-being, mentally and physically (and possibly spiritually too). But what has struck him most about a good many of what may be termed 'orthodox vegetarians' is their complete ignorance of the basic principles of sound dietetics, and the assumption (implied if not expressed) that they are a superior brand of mortal simply because they do not eat flesh foods and so refrain from contributing to the sufferings of the animal kingdom.

This 'holier than thou' attitude does no good to the vegetarian movement. It puts up the back of non-vegetarians and tends to make them hypercritical of vegetarianism as a whole, and is certainly not the way to make converts.

If certain vegetarians feel that the fact that they do not eat flesh foods confers on them some special moral superiority over meat-eaters, they can feel so if they wish, but it is hardly the type of attitude that will make them popular members of society. If one is a vegetarian for ethical reasons, then the fact that one is refraining from eating meat and inflicting pain on animals should be its own reward (apart from the physical benefits to be derived from a meatless diet if soundly arranged).

One should not continually regard oneself as a member of a class apart, a superior caste of beings who are constantly being contaminated and polluted by contact with ordinary mortals and their repulsive dietetic habits.

Of course, not all vegetarians are like this, but sufficient of them are for the need for this criticism to be voiced, and it is hoped that when this book has been fully studied many vegetarians as well as non-vegetarians will have found something of value in its pages.

There are quite a good many people these days who wish to become vegetarians, whether for ethical or health reasons, and do not know quite how to set about the task. They do not like to join any special vegetarian organization or feel they are becoming 'peculiar' in any way, and it is *especially* for this type of individual that this book is being written.

Being one of those people who do not like joining societies or groups himself, the author knows from personal experience that there is considerable need for guidance among such people. They feel they are playing a 'lone hand' and are rather at a loss to know just how to carry on.

It is sincerely hoped that this book will fill a long-felt need in this respect, as well as being of value to vegetarians generally and to those showing an intelligent interest in the subject (or who may wish to do so).

CHAPTER 1

BACKGROUND

Apart from those who are obliged to adopt a vegetarian diet for medical reasons, there are many people in Britain who are vegetarians by choice, and the number continues to grow year by year.

But, when the 'average' person hears that someone is a vegetarian he or she immediately assumes that there must be something peculiar about such an individual. Vegetarianism itself strikes them as peculiar, simply because it is something that runs contrary to accepted dietetic convention, and such people assume that because it is common to eat meat and flesh foods in this and other Western countries, therefore it is the 'normal' thing to do, and that all the world does likewise (and always did so).

Such folk would have quite a shock if they studied the dietetic habits of other races, climes and times. They would find that in India alone there are many many millions of people who have never included flesh foods in their diet since birth, and whose ancestors did not do so for thousands of years before them; whilst in other countries the eating of meat is quite uncommon and is often regarded as a 'luxury' for the rich.

Meat only became a common article of diet in these islands during the nineteenth century, when the 'free trade' policy of the Liberals brought large masses of flour, meat and other foods from markets overseas in exchange for the manufactured products of this country. Before the nineteenth century meat was far from being a common ingredient of the diet of the poorer sections of society, although the more well-to-do ate it freely. Among rustics meat was reserved for special occasions, and became, with the white bread which the rich used instead of the common wheaten bread of the populace, a symbol of wealth.

Yet the absence of meat from the diet of the peasants and artisans (or the rarity of its presence) did not make them any the less healthy than their more wealthy masters. The origin of the idea that 'meat confers strength' is difficult to discover, and it may be regarded as one of those convictions of thought that have grown up through the years without any real basis for their assumption.

THE MEAT MYTH

No one would regard the ancient Greek or Roman as lacking in strength, yet meat was far from a common ingredient in the diet of the less affluent of either country. The average Greek diet consisted of unleavened bread, figs, cheese, olives and garlic, meat being eaten only about once a week. The average Roman diet consisted of coarse porridge, peas, beans and lentils, cabbage, leeks and onions. Meat was eaten very occasionally. Yet both Greeks and Romans were unsurpassed for manly strength and endurance.

If we turn to modern times we shall find exactly the same thing. By common consent the healthiest race in the world are the Hunzas of North-West India. These hill-folk lead a hardy agricultural life, and disease is a great rarity among them. The men think nothing of running *sixty miles* a day over mountainous country, with a heavy load on their backs; and, all in all, they are the most handsome and virile race it is possible to see. Yet their diet is very similar to that of the ancient Greeks and Romans, consisting mainly of fruits and vegetables, whole-grain cereals, and milk products, with meat only consumed about once every ten days.

Thus the idea that meat is essential to health and strength is without any rational proof or foundation whatsoever, and the consensus of dietetic experience down the ages is ample refutation of it.

Whereas these races ate very little or no meat, they did not make any special virtue of the fact, or regard themselves as superior beings as a consequence. It was normal or natural for them to eat little or no meat, and that was the end of the matter.

But spiritually minded men and women from time immemorial have revolted against the idea of killing animals for food, with the attendant suffering and shedding of blood; many are the illustrious names that stud the pages of history who have exhorted people to embrace a non-flesh or vegetarian diet *on principle* (as opposed to mere necessity).

PAST PROTAGONISTS

The great sages who were responsible for the ancient Hindu Vedas were opposed to the shedding of blood, and the Lord Gautama (The Buddha) was opposed to the taking of life in any form. Pythagoras is an illustrious historical example of those who taught a vegetarian way of life, as also did Seneca and Plutarch.

The early Church Fathers, Clement of Alexandria and Tertullian, were both in favour of a meatless diet and wrote and preached on its behalf; whilst in more modern times we can cite the names of Swedenborg and John Wesley as ardent advocates of a vegetarian form of diet. Percy Bysshe Shelley will always be associated with vegetarianism, of which he was an ardent advocate, and the name of Jeremy Bentham has vegetarian associations as also that of John Howard, the pioneer of prison reform.

Count Tolstoy was an ardent vegetarian, of course, whilst the name of George Bernard Shaw will always be coupled with the subject in the public mind.

Thus has there been a long line of reformers down the ages who have advocated the avoidance of flesh foods because of the pain and suffering such a mode of diet inflicts on helpless animals; whilst at the same time there has been observed a marked improvement in the health of non-meat-eaters, provided their diet has been sensibly arranged to include all necessary food elements.

VEGETARIAN SOCIETIES

Vegetarianism as a movement gained momentum in Britain in the early part of the nineteenth century, and the English Vegetarian Society was founded in 1847 at Ramsgate. In the United States the impetus was even greater than in this country, and the names of a number of medical reformers have long been associated with the movement there, particularly such men as Doctors Trall, Kellogg and Jackson. Sylvester Graham, the pioneer of 'Graham Bread' (100% wholewheat bread), was one of the fathers of vegetarianism in the United States, and Horace Greely, the famous American, was one of its most ardent supporters.

Vegetarian societies have sprung up all over the world since those early days, and in this country many have devoted their lives to the spread of vegetarianism, some no doubt with more zeal than knowledge, it must be admitted. The name of Sir Isaac Pitman will always be associated with the vegetarian movement in this country, whilst among medical men the Allinsons have played their part in its advancement, as has Dr Josiah Oldfield, who lived to become a centenarian on his meatless dietary.

DIET REFORM

In the early days of this century the name of Eustace Miles came much to the fore in vegetarian circles, as a pioneer of 'diet reform' and healthy vegetarianism, as did later the name of Edgar Saxon.

These days there are vegetarian restaurants

and health food stores in most towns, and vegetarian journals and publications of all kinds continue to grow and flourish, as the number of groups and organizations within the vegetarian movement continues to increase.

I myself have never belonged to any vegetarian organizations, as I have an instinctive aversion to joining groups of any kind, but I have always admired the work of the vegetarian movement, in its attempts to spread the gospel of non-flesh-eating, although I have not always been in either sympathy or agreement with many of its views. At times I have even come into wordy conflict with some of its champions in the field of health journalism, and it has seemed to me that there is far too much narrow-mindedness and orthodoxy of outlook on the part of many vegetarians, especially those of the older generation.

These people seem to think that as long as an individual avoids all flesh, fish or fowl all his dietetic problems are automatically solved; but nothing could be further from the truth. Unless vegetarianism is pursued *intelligently* it can bring nothing but discredit upon the movement as a whole, and that the average non-vegetarian is only too ready to seize any available opportunity thus provided is common knowledge.

The bone of contention, therefore, between myself and the orthodox type of vegetarian, apart from the criticisms already briefly stated in the preface to this book, is the fact that I advocate a fusion between vegetarianism and real *diet reform*, whilst the orthodox vegetarian claims that vegetarianism is already identical to diet reform, and that the original founders of the vegetarian movement in this country were likewise the founders of diet reform too.

I beg to differ very strongly on this point, although I am only too ready to agree that many vegetarians were diet reformers (more or less instinctively), and some diet reform ideas were undoubtedly expounded by the early leaders of the vegetarian movement, with the most beneficial results. I refer here particularly to the idea of eating only 100% wholewheat bread, and the inclusion of plenty of salads and fruit in one's diet; but for all that, I feel compelled to aver that vegetarianism and diet reform are *not* identical, nor does the acceptance of vegetarianism automatically mean that one understands how best to arrange and balance the diet for health purposes. It is on this issue that I join conflict with orthodox vegetarians (in so far as there is any conflict).

CHAPTER 2

VEGETARIANISM AND DIET REFORM

It will be best to start this chapter with a definition of what we mean by the term *diet reform.* Diet reform (or food reform) signifies a movement designed to bring sensible and health-promoting ideas into the realm of conventional dietetics, based on sound physiological principles relative to the preparation, selection and arrangement of meals so as to ensure a really well-balanced and health-promoting dietary.

Diet reform as such has therefore nothing to do with vegetarianism, and indeed has sprung from an entirely different source, as I shall soon show; but it does happen that most diet reformers are also vegetarians. There are, however, diet reformers who are not and do not wish to be vegetarians, and who believe that the inclusion of a certain percentage of meat or other flesh foods in the dietary is not detrimental to health, so long as the diet as a whole is soundly balanced and arranged according to diet reform principles.

I have a certain amount of sympathy with this group of people, simply because it has never been my policy to try to force would-be diet reformers into embracing full vegetarianism if they do not wish to do so voluntarily; and in my own books and articles on diet and nature cure I have never sought to be dogmatic on the subject of not eating meat. I have left it to the reader to make up his or her own mind on the matter, after detailing what I think are the advantages of a fully vegetarian dietary. Coercion or pressure in such matters seems to me quite wrong. Each must decide for himself, after due consideration of all the facts.

Of course, if a person *wants* to be a vegetarian, nothing can prevent him from doing so; and we are not concerned with such folk at the moment. We are dealing with people who wish to reform their diet for *health reasons*, and the question of whether or not it is essential to become a vegetarian in order to achieve this. I have already said that, in my opinion, it is *not essential* to become a full vegetarian to be a diet reformer or food reformer, although I do feel that it is wisest to exclude flesh foods from the dietary for best results.

This is an issue every individual must decide for himself, therefore, and it is as well for would-be diet reformers to know in advance that in seeking to live on a more health-promoting dietary it is *not* necessary for them to embrace vegetarianism, although if they wish to do so, so much the better.

Orthodox vegetarians rather tend to confuse the issue here, as the whole crux of the matter with them is the giving up of meat and other flesh foods, by which they automatically assume that everything is being done to ensure the highest possible degree of health for the new convert to vegetarianism.

A STARCHY DIET

But many orthodox vegetarians know little or nothing about the principles of real diet reform, and if one should look over the type of diet they are accustomed to, one is appalled at its crudity and lack of balance. It is overburdened with cereal foods, nut and pulse dishes, and puddings and pastry, and even if the flour and cereals used are all 100% wholegrain, this does nothing to detract from the excessively starchy character of the diet, and its lack of proper dietetic balance. Fruits and salads are often conspicuous only by their absence.

Vegetarians of this sort are often far from healthy people as a result of their unwise feeding habits. It is from the ranks of such folk that arises the 'starch-poisoned' type of vegetarian, with pasty face, poor physique, and that caricature of health which non-vegetarians often delight in applying to *all* vegetarians.

Of course, many vegetarians are pictures of health and fitness (more so, in proportion to their numbers, than meat-eaters), and on balance they have a far better health record than non-vegetarians, as I hope to show later; but it is a fact that some vegetarians look the reverse of healthy, and it is from the class of vegetarian feeders described above that they are drawn more or less exclusively. This is simply because such people have no idea of real diet reform, or how to set about arranging a really well-balanced and health-promoting dietary, whilst at the same time remaining true to their vegetarian principles.

NATURE CURE MOVEMENT

Diet reform owes its inception and origin to the nature cure movement, nature cure being a system of disease-treatment which depends for its results mainly on fasting, strict dieting, and the proper use of fresh air, sunshine, exercise, water, and other natural health-promoting agencies.

Through fasting and dieting many sufferers from the most diverse kinds of chronic ailments have been restored to health under nature cure treatment, and it is essentially to the nature cure school that diet reform belongs. They have developed diet reform as part of their technique of treatment of their cases and, although in most nature cure establishments and under most naturopaths, the importance of not eating meat is emphasized (especially in cases of rheumatism, arthritis, and other similar chronic maladies), it is by no means part of the nature cure philosphy to seek to turn everyone into a strict vegetarian.

Most naturopaths are vegetarians by choice, but there is no hard-and-fast union between nature cure and vegetarianism, or between diet reform (which, as just explained, is a direct offshoot of nature cure) and vegetarianism.

Many of the original nature cure pioneers were strict vegetarians themselves, and a fleshless diet has long been advocated as the best for health in nature cure literature; but if the reader bears these facts in mind he will not fall into the error, made by many vegetarians themselves, of assuming (without any reason at all) that vegetarianism and diet reform are synonymous.

To practise diet reform one must understand its basic principles, and these can be summarized briefly as follows:

1. Seeing that 75% to 80% of the total bulk of food eaten consists of fresh fruits and salads and conservatively cooked vegetables (preferably compost grown) so as to ensure that the diet as a whole has an *alkaline* and not an *acid* reaction in the system (as has the conventional diet of meat, white bread, white sugar, tinned foods and badly cooked vegetables).
2. Seeing that all bread, flour, sugar and cereals come from 100% natural sources, and have not been refined, processed or tampered with in any way before using.
3. Seeing that tinned and processed foods are avoided and that such things as cakes, puddings, pastry, jams, custards, jellies, and other artificial comestibles are kept down to a minimum and always prepared from the ingredients referred to in (2) above.
4. Seeing that such accessories as condiments, sauces and seasonings, tea and coffee (which have an unhealthy stimulating effect on the digestive tract and system generally) are kept out of the diet to ensure maximum benefit from the food eaten.

TEA AND COFFEE

With regard to tea and coffee, not every diet reformer is prepared to give up these drinks entirely, and if taken in small quantities and very weak they can be included in the diet with very little harm. But many orthodox vegetarians consume tea and coffee in excessive amounts, and have a very generous attitude towards condiments, sauces and seasonings, to say nothing of their predilection for stodgy cheese and nut and pulse dishes, and heavy puddings and pies of all kinds.

Thus, the principles of true diet reform are far from being adhered to by many vegetarians, especially as regards the inclusion of 75% to 80% fruit and vegetables in the dietary. Many 'orthodox' vegetarians fight shy of fresh fruit and salads, and much prefer to have their vegetables prepared and cooked in the ordinary conventional way instead of steaming them. Thus, on balance, their food habits are not very much different from those of the average meat-eater, except that they leave out all flesh foods and presumably use wholewheat bread instead of white, and wholewheat flour for making puddings and pastry.

This can hardly be called diet reform by any stretch of the imagination and, as already indicated, such vegetarians are often far from healthy-looking specimens of humanity and are no credit to the movement. When non-vegetarians want to disparage vegetarianism they are always on the look-out for vegetarians of this category, to compare with really healthy-looking meat-eaters, and vegetarians as a whole do not come out favourably from the comparison.

Of course, there are countless numbers of meat-eaters who are in a deplorable state of health (and who fill our hospitals and infirmaries to overflowing), but it is only natural for non-vegetarians to seek to compare their best with the worst that vegetarianism can show; and until *all* vegetarians understand and practise real diet reform there will always be plenty of opportunity for non-vegetarians to point laughingly and accusingly at what some vegetarians look like. It is unfair but it is all too human, and vegetarians have themselves largely to blame for this state of affairs.

I have already dealt comprehensively with the whole question of diet reform in my book *Your Diet in Health and Disease*, first published in 1931 and still much in demand in the field of health literature; and to that volume readers must be referred if they wish to know more about the subject than can be provided in the small compass of this book.

Meantime I trust I have made the main difference between vegetarianism and diet reform clear to those who have hitherto not understood the full distinction between them, and before the end of this book I shall give a general idea of how best to arrange a vegetarian dietary in full conformity with diet reform principles.

Such a dietary can provide nothing but the best of health for those adopting it, for it is based on the soundest of hygienic laws, as proved over many years by the nature cure school in the treatment of many varieties of chronic ailments by naturopaths and in nature cure homes.

Having removed this misunderstanding, or possible misunderstanding, we are now free to go forward with the fuller examination of the subject and, accordingly, the next chapter will deal with some of the popular misconceptions common to non-vegetarians about meat-eating and non-meat-eating.

CHAPTER 3

SOME POPULAR MISCONCEPTIONS

The stock argument of the non-vegetarian when thinking or talking about vegetarianism is that one cannot be healthy without including meat in the diet. In some mysterious and indeed mystical way meat is supposed to be the only food that can build virile health and provide the individual with a full supply of rich, red blood.

But if one takes a look at the animal kingdom it is soon seen that the animals who do the heaviest work and are the strongest and hardiest are all non-flesh-feeders, such as the horse, ox, elephant and rhinoceros. The rhinoceros and elephant are two of the strongest animals, and even if we include the gorilla in this category, it too is a non-flesh-eater, living exclusively on wild fruits, nuts and edible shoots.

The lion and tiger are the two best-known examples of flesh-eating animals but, although so merciless and powerful, for sheer strength and endurance they have to give way to the three animals just cited; so that it by no means follows that a flesh dietary is essential either to strength or health in the sub-human world.

Turning from the animal to the human kingdom, examples have already been given of races and peoples who have maintained a very high degree of health on a diet either entirely or almost entirely lacking in meat or other flesh foods, so that it is difficult to see how this legend about the necessity for meat in the diet can be maintained. It survives only through sheer prejudice and 'wishful thinking', although many medical men subscribe to this fetish of meat-eating for health, and seek to persuade the general public that without meat in the diet one cannot possibly be really healthy.

WARTIME RATIONING

But the rationing experience we in England went through during the war years is ample proof itself that meat is not an essential ingredient of a health-promoting diet. As a result of rationing we saw the meat allowance drastically cut, yet, far from the health of the nation deteriorating as a result, as one would expect if all this hullaballoo about meat-eating were true, *it actually improved*!

Thus, from this one elementary example alone, it is obvious that plenty of meat in the diet is *not* essential for health, and a nation is actually far healthier the less its people consume meat as a regular feature of their daily dietary.

This fact has also been borne out in other countries under the exigency of war. In Denmark, during the 1914-18 war, the population had to subsist on a meatless diet, but according to official statistics they emerged from their 'ordeal' a far healthier race than before the war, when meat and other flesh foods were plentiful.

Of course, the credit for this result has to go to Dr Hindhede, the great Danish food scientist, for it was his understanding of the principles of correct nutrition that enabled the Danish people to come through so creditably. The same thing happened during World War II in Switzerland, according to the evidence of Dr Fleisch, who looked after the diet of the Swiss people during the war years. Here too there was a minimum consumption of flesh foods, but a maximum consumption of vegetables and whole-grain cereal products, and the health of the Swiss people was greatly enhanced as a result of this enforced adoption of diet reform principles. In commenting on the matter in scientific journals, Dr Fleisch agrees with the nature cure school that orthodox dietitians grossly over-estimate the body's need for proteins, starches, sugars and fats.

In the case of thousands of individuals under nature cure treatment the exclusion of meat from the diet has resulted in greatly improved health, when the dietary as a whole has conformed to diet reform standards; yet, despite these self-evident truths, people as a whole still believe implicitly in the legend that meat is essential to health and that without it one cannot possibly have a sufficiency of red, rich blood in one's arteries!

Of course, such people do not *want* to be convinced that one can live healthily without meat, and that is the whole crux of the situation.

NEED FOR PROTEIN

Coming down to a more scientific examination of our subject, what precisely is it that is supposed to confer such a special virtue on meat as a food? It is a *protein* food, and proteins are essential for the upkeep, growth and repair of the fleshy parts of our bodies, also of the vital organs and blood-vessels. It is also from proteins that blood is made and the many body secretions, glandular extracts and digestive ferments are elaborated.

Thus it is readily seen that proteins are absolutely essential to life, let alone health. But is meat the *only* protein? Far from it. There are many other protein foods besides meat, such as fish, milk, cheese, eggs and nuts; whilst pulses such as beans, peas and lentils also contain a fair percentage of protein, especially the *soya bean.* All cereals contain quite a considerable percentage of protein too, and fruits and vegetables yield small amounts of protein also. Thus many categories of food contain protein, and some actually contain more protein than meat itself!

It is absurd, therefore, to assume that without meat the protein requirements of the body cannot be met. If one knows which foods to substitute in its place in the diet, one can be sure of providing the system with all the protein it needs for its effective and efficient functioning and, what is most important from the health point of view, the protein will be obtained from a less toxic source than meat.

ACID/ALKALI BALANCE

Meat and fish and other flesh foods are notoriously toxin-forming, because they putrefy so readily in the intestines after consumption (if not already in a partially putrefactive state before being eaten); to say nothing of the fact that such foods are very acid-forming in character also.

With the general exception of fresh ripe fruits and vegetables and milk, every class of food tends to produce an acid reaction in the tissues after digestion and assimilation, and this acid refuse left in the tissues tends to accumulate through the years, if the diet as a whole contains a preponderance of such acid-forming foods (as is the case with the conventional meat, white sugar, white bread, pudding, pastry, strong tea diet), thus paving the way for most of the common diseases of our day.

Such diseases are *not* due to germs, although germs may play a superficial part in their development in certain instances; and it is because, under nature cure treatment, this fact is fully realized, that so much can be done to cure sufferers from chronic diseases of all kinds by fasting and dietetic measures which tend to get rid of this over-acid state of the tissues and bring about a proper acid-alkaline balance.

Many sufferers from chronic disease, after having been given up by medical science as incurable, have made dramatic improvement in health simply by being put on a fast and/or fruit and vegetable diet, because in that way the acid condition of their tissues has been rapidly reduced, this over-acid state being the true cause of their chronic ill-health.

Thus, under nature cure treatment, it is the over-acidity of the tissues that receives main attention, because this is the main causative agent at work in the production of disease. It will therefore be realized by the reader that the avoidance of meat and other highly acid-forming foods is essential for best and speediest results.

Also, where meat and other highly concentrated proteins have been consumed in excess of bodily need, the excess has to be broken down by the liver and excreted via the kidneys. A high-protein meat diet is therefore a great strain on the liver and kidneys, and directly contributes towards the disease of those organs.

It may thus be said that over-consumption of meat and other flesh foods is an incentive towards the development of disease in the human system, and such foods must be kept down to a very low level indeed, and combined with plenty of alkaline fruits and vegetables, to keep the necessary acid-alkaline balance for clean healthy tissues, a condition synonymous with *health*.

In no other way can the human body be really healthy and able to function at optimum efficiency. The next chapter will include some comparative data relative to the acid-forming propensities of meat and other protein foods, as well as other facts relative to such foods which will demonstrate clearly that the less we include flesh proteins in the diet, the better for health in every way.

With regard to that ancient shibboleth that unless we consume plenty of meat we shall become bloodless and anaemic, the facts prove that this is not the case at all. *All* protein foods help to produce blood (in conjunction with the body's own metabolic processes), and proteins such as eggs, cheese, nuts, pulses and milk can do this far more healthily than meat, when taken as part of a balanced reformed dietary on nature cure lines.

If one does not include in the diet a proper percentage of protein of reliable value to replace meat and other flesh foods, then one *will* become anaemic and bloodless, but this only happens when the person concerned has no knowledge of food values at all, and persists in excluding *all* protein food from the diet for an extended period.

NUTRITIVE VALUE

Medical circles have claimed that vegetable proteins such as nuts and pulses are not equal in either nutritive value or body-building power to proteins from animal sources. Even if this is true to some extent, if one includes eggs, cheese and milk in the diet (as most vegetarians do) the protein from these sources is equal in value to anything obtainable from flesh foods, and is less toxic in content. These are 'first-class' proteins in every sense of the word, as good as anything that may come from flesh-food sources. It is only the very ignorant who imagine that vegetarians do not eat eggs and dairy products such as milk, cheese, butter and cream as part of their vegetarian diet.

The idea that vegetarians are persons who live just on nuts and vegetables is something suitable only for comedy; it may give meat-eaters a laugh, but it has no foundation in fact. But many vegetarians certainly do not make the fullest possible use of modern dietetic knowledge in planning their dietary, as was shown in the last chapter. Hence the need for a reformation of ideas among many vegetarians, as well as among meat-eaters, in the best interests of the health of the body.

To sum up this chapter, therefore, there is not the faintest vestige of scientific evidence to show that meat and other flesh foods are essential to health; one can keep in optimum health on a meatless dietary as long as one knows how to arrange the dietary to include all necessary food elements and preserve the acid-alkaline balance.

There is much evidence to show that meat-eating contributes towards the development of disease, especially chronic disease, if consumed in excess. Diseases of a rheumatic nature are especially related to a meat-eating régime of living, because of the excessively acid-forming character of such foods (as also are liver and kidney disorders and diseases of the blood-vessels such as arterio-sclerosis and its concomitant high blood-pressure).

Where constipation is present (as it usually is on the conventional dietary of meat, white bread, white sugar, boiled vegetables), the possible results are far more serious than when one is living on a vegetarian diet. This is because the bowel contents in the former case are highly putrefactive, whereas the bowel content on a vegetarian type of diet is not so. It is more fermentative than putrefactive. The fact that some vegetarians do suffer from constipation is itself a sign that they do not know how to properly arrange their diet for themselves; because under diet reform constipation is very rapidly banished because of the large daily intake of fruit and vegetables.

Thus, on all counts, a meatless diet has the advantage over a diet containing meat, despite present-day prejudice and misunderstanding, and the facts to be revealed in the next chapter will amply endorse this statement.

CHAPTER 4

FACTS ABOUT ANIMAL AND NON-ANIMAL PROTEINS

Following the remarks at the end of the previous chapter, the reader is invited to take note of the following facts relative to animal and non-animal proteins obtained from *The Chemical Composition of Foods*, by McCance and Widdowson, a standard work on nutritional values. The first group concerns protein composition, and the following table speaks for itself:—

Food	*Percentage Protein*	*Percentage Fat*
Bacon, gammon, fried	31.3	33.9
Bacon, streaky, fried	24.0	46.0
Beef, sirloin, roast, lean and fat	21.3	32.1
Beef steak, fried	20.4	20.4
Chicken, boiled	26.2	10.3
Duck, roast	22.8	23.6
Ham, boiled	16.3	39.6
Mutton chop, grilled	19.9	45.0
Pork, leg, roast	24.6	23.2
Turkey, roast	30.2	7.7
Veal cutlet, fried	30.4	8.1
Cod, steamed	18.0	0.9
Haddock, fresh, steamed	22.0	0.8
Herring, fried	21.8	15.1
Lemon sole, steamed	19.9	0.9
Plaice, steamed	18.1	1.9
Salmon, fresh, steamed	19.1	13.0
Trout, steamed	22.3	4.5
Cheese, Cheddar	24.9	34.5
Cheese, Dutch	28.1	16.8
Cheese, Gruyère	36.8	33.4
Cheese, Stilton	25.1	40.0
Egg yolk	16.2	30.5
Eggs, poached	12.4	11.7
Milk, fresh, whole	3.3	3.7
Milk, dried, whole	26.4	29.7
Almonds	20.5	53.5
Barcelona nuts	12.9	64.0
Brazil nuts	13.8	61.5
Peanuts	28.1	49.0
Walnuts	12.5	51.5

Food	*Percentage Protein*	*Percentage Fat*
Beans, baked	6.0	0.4
Beans, haricot, boiled	6.6	Trace
Lentils, boiled	6.8	Trace
Peas, fresh, boiled	5.0	Trace
Peas, split, dried, boiled	8.3	Trace
Wholemeal flour (92%)	15.3	3.1
Wholemeal bread (92%)	10.8	2.2
Soya flour	40.3	23.5

A glance over this table will show the reader at once that there are quite a number of protein foods richer in protein and valuable fats than flesh foods, and it will be seen that cheese forms the best source of animal protein food available, weight for weight with all other proteins, animal or non-animal.

I have already spoken about the highly acid-forming character of flesh foods, and perhaps the following table – taken from the book previously mentioned – will make this point more clear to the reader.

ACID-BASE BALANCE OF FOODS, C.C. PER 100 GRAMS

Food	*N/ 10 Acid*	*N/ 10 Alkaline*
Bacon, gammon, fried	408	
Bacon, streaky, fried	170	
Beef, sirloin, roast	190	
Beef steak, fried	173	
Chicken, boiled	207	
Duck, roast	244	

Food	*N/10 Acid*	*N/10 Alkaline*
Ham, boiled	162	
Mutton chop, grilled	141	
Pork, leg, roast	286	
Turkey, roast	195	
Veal cutlet, fried	235	
Cod, steamed	162	
Haddock, steamed	177	
Herring, fried	219	
Lemon sole, steamed	194	
Plaice, steamed	184	
Salmon, fresh, steamed	162	
Trout, steamed	152	
Cheese, Cheddar	54	
Cheese, Dutch		59
Cheese, Gruyère		36
Cheese, Stilton	78	
Egg yolk	332	
Eggs, poached	197	
Milk, fresh, whole		27
Milk, dried, whole		216
Almonds		183
Barcelona nuts		182
Brazil nuts		45
Peanuts	116	
Walnuts	84	
Beans, baked		28
Beans, haricot, boiled		50
Lentils, boiled		4
Peas, fresh, boiled	14	
Peas, split, dried, boiled	5	
Wholemeal flour (92%)	84	
Wholemeal bread (92%)	48	

A glance at this table will reveal at once that a dietary that makes up its protein requirements from cheese, milk, pulses and nuts is actually alkaline on balance (or very nearly so), whereas those who use flesh foods for protein are consuming a very high acid-forming fare. The acid forming propensity is greatly enhanced by the consumption of white bread, white sugar, and other processed and refined foods in the dietary. Thus the vegetarian who plans his diet wisely is again much better off, from the all-round health point of view, than the average meat-eater, and only ignorance and wilful refusal to face the facts would deny these statements.

VITAMIN SUPPLIES

Now let us examine the matter again from a different angle. It is assumed that meat and other flesh foods are essential to the diet because they are rich in vitamin B. The following facts taken from *Food Values at a Glance*, by Violet G. Plimmer, will soon explode this idea.

She gives the following foods in order of richness of vitamin B 1:

Dried yeast; yeast extracts; wheat germ products; dried peas, beans, lentils; nuts; wholemeal wheat and barley; rye, oatmeal and maize; natural brown rice; lean of pork, ham, bacon, liver, heart, kidney, fish roe; fruits and vegetables; lean meat.

It will be noted that meat comes very low down on this list of foods rich in vitamin B 1. Now let us turn to foods rich in vitamin B 2 complex. We find these, in order of richness, given as follows:

Dried yeast; yeast extract; liver, heart, kidney; lean meat; fish; wheat germ; whole rice; bran; milk, egg yolk; tomatoes.

Thus flesh foods are far from being the best and only sources of this vitamin, and a balanced diet on food reform lines, containing wholewheat bread and wholegrain cereals and dairy products, will be found to supply all the vitamin B requirements of the body amply.

Now let us turn to the question of iron. We are told by medical men that meat is rich in iron, and that is one of the reasons why it should be included in the diet. But let us see which are actually the best sources for the provision of iron in the dietary. From the book just mentioned we are given the following data.

The foods richest in iron, in order of richness, are:

Lentils, egg yolk; liver; dried beans; black treacle; oysters, oatmeal; dried peas; wholewheat; dried currants; almonds; lean beef; turnip-top greens; spinach; raisins; dates; eggs, olives; dandelion greens; dried figs; prunes; chocolate; Scotch kale; green peas; peanuts; lean pork; asparagus; bacon; broccoli; cheese.

Is meat therefore necessary for the provision of iron in the diet? Most decidedly not if these facts have any validity, and please note that they are taken from a standard text-book on the subject.

When we consider other essential food minerals such as calcium, phosphorus and potassium, we shall find that the vegetarian can secure far more ample supplies of these from his diet than the meat-eater, so long as he sees that he eats only wholewheat bread, wholegrain cereals, and natural unrefined foods generally in his vegetarian dietary. Any table of comparative analyses will prove this fact up to the hilt. The only outstanding scientific point still remaining, therefore, regarding the protein needs for the body, is this question of 'first-class' versus 'second-class' protein.

AMINO ACIDS

Orthodox dietitians have insisted for a long time that only protein from animal sources is first-class protein, because it contains all the amino-acids required by the body for its many and varied needs. These same dietetic experts have stated categorically that protein from vegetable sources, such as nuts, grains, pulses, and fruits and vegetables, is only second-class protein because it does not contain all the amino-acids. (It should be explained here that all proteins are broken down into these amino-acids after digestion, and become the building-bricks of the body for use in the tasks of growth, reconstruction and repair of tissue, organs and blood. in the tasks of growth, reconstruction and repair of tissues, organs and blood.) It is true that protein from vegetable sources does not contain every amino-acid in every separate case, but when we take a *mixture* of such vegetable proteins, what may be lacking in one is made up from another, so that *on balance* we can obtain *all* the necessary amino-acids from a *mixed* vegetarian diet, especially if such a diet contains animal proteins as well, such as eggs, cheese and milk (as is the case with the great majority of vegetarians). Thus the case against the vegetarian falls to the ground here too, on analysis, and we are left with the impression that only a sort of mystic belief in the value and virtue of meat imbues the detractors of a vegetarian mode of dietary. At least, that is the only conclusion the unbiased observer can come to after a study of the facts presented (from authentic scientific sources) in this chapter.

CHAPTER 5

HUMANITARIAN, HYGIENIC AND PHYSIOLOGICAL ASPECTS

Having studied the vegetarian question from the purely dietetic angle, and shown that it is far more health-promoting than the conventional flesh-food dietary, let us now examine the matter from other points of view. Let us begin with the *humanitarian* aspect.

From the purely humanitarian standpoint the vegetarian wins all along the line. Indeed, it is this aspect of the matter that is usually stressed most in vegetarian literature, and was one of the chief reasons why vegetarianism, as a movement, came into being.

People were appalled at the suffering inflicted upon dumb creatures in killing them for human consumption as food, and although the slaughtering of animals these days is far less cruel than it used to be, there is nothing so edifying to the conscience as a visit to a slaughterhouse. If the erstwhile interested visitor can leave the scene with anything but horror and repulsion in his breast, then he must be a very strange and heartless being indeed.

It is safe to say that the vast majority of meat-eaters only keep on doing so because they do not see slaughtered the animals that they consume. If they were compelled to see, only once, the conditions under which the animals are brought to the *abattoirs* for slaughter, and the actual conditions of slaughter, it is safe to assume there would be a vast increase in the numbers of vegetarians overnight! No sensitive human being can condone such sights, smells and sounds once having experienced them.

It is safe to say there would be very few meat-eaters if they had to consume their meat raw. It is only cooking that has made meat-eating palatable (and much of the food-value of the meat is lost in the process!).

HYGIENE

From the *hygienic* point of view it is obvious that if the slaughtering of animals for food was done away with, a potential source of municipal contamination would automatically be removed. The evils associated with the killing of animals for food seep into the life of society in ways often little appreciated, and I submit that the health of communities is often lowered (especially in hot weather) by the presence of slaughterhouses in their midst.

It stands to reason that this must be so, when one considers the concomitants of the killing process (the blood, sweat, urine, dung, hides and offal) which are often allowed to partially decompose and decay before removal, and the hordes of flies and other pests attracted to such scenes.

Then the *fear* engendered in the animals themselves, when they smell the blood and effluvia left by their predecessors on coming near the environs of the *abattoir*, is something that has to be considered from the hygienic angle too. This fear not only contaminates the actual carcasses after slaughter, it is an emanation that pervades and hangs about the whole place, and is something almost *tangible* to those who have visited such spots. This psychic aura of fear and death must inevitably pollute the surrounding atmosphere, and in turn will contribute towards epidemics and outbreaks of disease of various kinds.

Hygienically we must also consider the effect of their work on the men who do the actual slaughtering. Not only does such an occupation deprave and coarsen such men, it also tends to make them more prone to drunkenness and disease than people doing other types of work, as official statistics show. Thus nature exacts her toll for such activities, whether we are conscious of the fact or not.

When we consider the *physiological* aspects of the subject there are one or two points that need noting. The first is that because he has such a large intestinal tract it is obvious that nature did not intend man to eat flesh foods. Flesh-eating animals always have a very short gut (intestinal tract) because of the highly putrefactive character of the food they eat. Nature tries to keep possible internal infection from such sources to a minimum, hence the short gut.

PUTREFACTION RISK

Man has a large intestinal tract, and therefore the risks from putrefaction are considerably enhanced on a meat-eating dietary, especially if constipation is present. Then again, a study of man's teeth shows us that he was not intended to be a meat-eater, because all *carnivores* are provided with special teeth for tearing and rending the flesh from their victims. Man's physiological make-up, in short, tends to the belief that he was designed for a frugivorous mode of dietary, like the apes and monkeys, although later he became omnivorous in dietetic habits.

It is not denied that man can keep healthy on a dietary containing meat, *but only if flesh foods are kept to a minimum, and the rest of the diet is on strict food reform lines.* Otherwise his dietary inevitably tends towards the production of disease in one form or another.

It is hoped that the points stressed in this chapter have made the reader appreciate the wide number of other aspects of the matter in which the vegetarian comes out superior to the meat-eater on balance.

CHAPTER 6

REMARKS ON VEGANISM, GUEST HOUSES AND VEGETARIAN ATHLETES

People who become vegetarians for humanitarian and ethical reasons should logically not consume animal products of any kind, as these are presumably obtained from animal sources through the infliction of some form of pain or coercion.

At least that is the standpoint adopted by those extremists among vegetarians who call themselves *vegans.* These people omit all animal produce from their diet, refusing to take eggs, cheese, milk, butter, cream or honey, as these are all of animal origin.

Of course, as already pointed out, most vegetarians do eat such animal produce, and if the number of vegetarians in existence was confined to those who have embraced *veganism*, I am afraid there would be very few indeed to uphold the vegetarian movement.

I agree that logically the vegans are right in refusing to eat animal produce of any kind in their vegetarian diet, as they have adopted a vegetarian régime of living for strictly humanitarian and ethical reasons, and their chief concern is the pain and suffering inflicted upon animals.

No doubt in keeping cows for milking, and hens for laying eggs, human beings do inflict a certain amount of pain, discomfort and perhaps even suffering on the cows and hens, and tend to shorten their lives. We know also that to get honey from the hive many bee-keepers force the bees to exist on white sugar during the winter months, which is definitely an unnatural practice.

RIGHT IN PRINCIPLE

Thus the vegan is undoubtedly right in principle in refraining from eating any article of food from animal sources, having regard to the reason for his adoption of a vegetarian dietary in the first place. But it is extremely debatable whether it is possible to maintain full health on a diet that excludes milk, cheese, eggs, butter and honey, at least in a climate such as we experience in this country.

It may be possible, and many vegans claim that they do; but some vegans I have known personally certainly do not seem able to do so, and more than one has had to give up his veganism and return to a more conventional vegetarian diet which does include animal produce.

If one wishes to maintain full health on a vegan diet, one would have to know a great deal about food values and how to arrange and combine the dietary to ensure a full intake of all essential food elements; and I personally doubt whether all vegans have the requisite dietetic knowledge required for the task. If people are going to fall into sub-health merely on a question of principle, I personally feel it is time to draw the line there.

After all, the taking of life is part of the process of existence, and so are the reception and infliction of pain; but that is no reason why we should *consciously and wilfully* seek to take life or inflict pain ourselves, either on human beings or animals. That is the whole ethical basis of vegetarianism.

When our principles in this direction tend to militate against our own health and well-being, as they may well do if one adopts veganism without a thorough understanding of what one is doing, then we are reaching a position of absurdity from which it is time to withdraw in our own best interests. Otherwise we are just making a sacrifice of ourselves for the benefit of the animal kingdom. This means that we are reversing the whole order of *evolution*, by making the higher serve the lower, instead of *vice versa.*

COMMON-SENSE

I am fully aware that this whole question can be hotly debated for hours on end, and there is no doubt that there are many rabid vegans who would regard what has been said here as sheer sacrilege. But I feel that at bottom it is entirely a question of *common-sense*, and it seems rather ridiculous to risk sacrificing one's health simply to support a principle which, although logical, yet is an entirely extremist viewpoint.

The world is already suffering greatly from the actions and views of extremists of various kinds, so why add more fuel to the fire? To those vegans who feel they are able to keep 100% healthy on their mode of diet, I say 'good luck'! To those who are unable to do so, I say 'modify your principles and revert to the more ordinary vegetarian dietary in order to be able to perform your allotted task in the world!'

VEGETARIAN GUEST HOUSES

Having got that off my chest, I must say a few words about vegetarian guest houses. This is a subject about which I feel rather strongly, as it has been my misfortune from time to time to have come into contact with such places where the fare provided did a great disservice to the whole cause of vegetarianism.

It needs to be stressed that if one wishes to make vegetarianism attractive, and to make new converts, the food and catering facilities at vegetarian hotels and guest houses should be of the highest culinary standard. If this standard is not kept to, guests may well go away with the feeling: 'if *this* is vegetarianism, give me normal food every time!'

But to be quite fair, I must admit that I have found plenty of vegetarian guest houses where the food was delectable and on the best diet reform lines.

HOLIDAY FOOD

I am not one of those people who place food first when going on holiday, but I do submit that it is a very important item, and can make or mar a holiday in many instances. I feel, therefore, that in the best interests of the vegetarian movement all vegetarian guest houses should be registered, and only those capable of providing a satisfactory standard of food reform catering should be permitted to call themselves *diet reform* . —

There are some vegetarian restaurants in existence that could also benefit by a knowledge of attractive diet reform. It would greatly enhance their service and attract many new customers to them. The old stodgy vegetarianism is fast dying, and in its place we want something far more enticing and palatable dietetically – something based on *sound diet reform principles*!

Indeed, in recent years the number of vegetarian restaurants has increased considerably and the standards of service and catering in many of them are a credit to the movement. It is imperative, therefore, that everything possible should be done to prevent the shortcomings of a minority from bringing the whole movement into disrepute.

VEGETARIAN ATHLETES

Despite the fact that many thousands of people have achieved a far higher standard of health on a vegetarian diet than on one containing flesh foods, and despite the facts and arguments put forward in this book on behalf of a meatless dietary for health and fitness, there are still many, no doubt, who cannot believe it possible that one can sustain maximum strength on a diet lacking in meat.

The best answer on this point can be provided by the performances of vegetarian athletes. There is surely nothing that requires more physical fitness and stamina than athletics; so that if vegetarians can hold their own with meat-eaters in athletic events, this must undoubtedly silence all criticism on the question of whether it is possible to secure maximum physical strength and endurance on a meatless dietary.

OLYMPIAN FEATS

Members of the Vegetarian Cycling and Athletic Club have been chosen many times to represent the country in the Olympic Games. These games are, in effect, the world amateur championships, and the Club has provided both winners and second and third placings over the years. Vegetarians, both members and non-members of the Club, have in fact had remarkable successes in national and world competition.

On a more personal note, the writer himself, although no athlete, has for years often walked more than twenty miles on a Sunday, on his country rambles, on a simple fruit and salad diet that many people might think insufficient to feed a child of six. Yet he is able to return home with no undue fatigue, and can out-distance many non-vegetarians on such trips, and in walking generally.

He does not put these facts forward as an example of his special prowess as a walker; far from it. It is merely to show that it is quite easy to walk long distances on a meatless dietary, and with less fatigue than many meat-eaters would experience.

CHAPTER 7

PREPARING A HEALTHFUL VEGETARIAN DIET

It is now time to get to grips with the more practical aspects of this book, which are, in effect, to explain to the reader how to prepare a healthful vegetarian dietary for himself.

It is easy enough to become a vegetarian by giving up all flesh foods, but it is quite another thing to know how to balance one's meals to ensure maximum health on a meatless dietary. It is safe to say that many honest and sincere vegetarians go through life with but the haziest idea of what they are doing in this respect, and it says much for the human constitution that it can stand up so well to the food foibles of some vegetarians I have known.

It is not sufficient just to leave flesh foods out of the dietary; for maximum health the diet as a whole must be based on diet reform principles. An idea of what those principles are has already been given in Chapter 2. What we have to do is to ensure an optimum daily intake of all essential food elements, including the organic mineral salts and vitamins; and to that end we should proceed as follows:

Make it an unvarying rule to have a large salad every day, summer and winter alike. During winter one can use shredded heart of cabbage or savoy instead of lettuce, and grated raw carrot and beetroot, onion and anything else in the raw vegetable line available. Such a salad can have a little grated cheese over if wished, or some milled nuts, and some olive oil and a squeeze of lemon juice as dressing.

With the salad one should have wholewheat bread, toast or crispbread, and butter or margarine perhaps with a yeast extract. Some vegetable soup can be taken before such a salad meal if desired, and as desert one can have fresh, stewed or dried fruit, or a baked apple or junket, or a piece of wholemeal cake.

One meal should consist of conservatively cooked vegetables (or another raw salad if preferred); with which one should have an egg dish or cheese dish or a vegetarian savoury of some kind, which will be the vegetarian equivalent of the meat other people eat at their cooked meal. As dessert one can have something along the lines of the dessert course given for the salad meal, or an occasional portion of wholemeal pudding.

FRUIT FOR BREAKFAST

The breakfast meal should be a fruit meal where possible, such as fresh and dried fruit and milk or nuts. If fresh fruit is not available one can have stewed or bottled fruit instead, or a crisp cereal or grated raw carrot as alternatives, with wheat germ or bran product.

Or one can have muesli. This is made by soaking overnight one or two tablespoons of raw porridge oats in sufficient milk or water to cover. Then, in the morning, add one large grated apple or a grated carrot, or a small cup of chopped fruit of some kind, fresh or dried, and a little lemon or orange juice and honey. When ready to serve a little more milk may be added, or cream if available.

A dietary of three meals a day such as this will ensure maximum health and fitness, and at night one can have a drink of vegetable soup or broth if wished, or a hot lemon drink, or a milky drink of some kind, and fruit and vegetable drinks can be taken during the day as wished. Tea as a definite meal is not advised, although a cup or two of weak China tea can be taken during the afternoon if desired.

The best thing for cooking vegetables is a *pressure cooker* or a casserole, and all liquid should be preserved and used as a vegetable drink, flavoured with a yeast extract if wished.

Items to be avoided are: white sugar, jams, marmalade; strong tea and coffee; condiments, sauces and seasonings; white bread and white-flour products of all kinds; milk puddings and pastry.

For seasoning one can use herbs of various kinds if desired, and natural brown sugar or treacle or honey should be used for sweetening. Dandelion coffee should be used instead of ordinary coffee.

In general, tinned foods should *not* be consumed, although tinned fruits and vegetables, or fruit and vegetable juices, are permissible when fresh fruit and vegetables are scarce. Frozen foods are also permissible at such times. On rising one can have a fruit drink of some kind.

QUANTITIES

As regards quantities of food, let hunger be the guide always. If fruit and vegetables form the bulk of each meal, as suggested, there need be no fear of over-eating the more concentrated proteins, starches, sugars and fats, so long as common discretion is observed. Never be afraid to miss a meal (or even two or three meals) if not hungry. It is a great mistake to imagine one must always eat at usual meal-times even when no appetite is present.

An occasional fast for a day or two is good for everyone, and one can make a habit of fasting for two or three days every six to eight weeks or so with the greatest benefit to one's general health and fitness. Eat slowly and masticate all food thoroughly in the mouth, and do not engage in any arduous physical exercise directly after a meal. Never eat when over-tired or emotionally upset. Food eaten on such occasions does far more harm than good.

SPECIMEN MENU

To those who follow these simple dietetic rules nothing but good can result, as proved by the author himself as well as thousands of other followers of a diet reform régime. For fuller information on the subject of diet reform in general, the reader is referred to the author's book *Your Diet in Health and Disease*, already mentioned. Those wishing to obtain some very useful recipes on diet reform lines can be confidently referred to *Everywoman's Wholefood Cook Book* by Vivien and Clifford Quick.

The following specimen menu will, however, serve as a guide in planning a healthful dietary:

On rising Fruit drink or rose hip syrup or blackcurrant syrup.

Breakfast Fresh and dried fruit and milk or nuts; or muesli; or grated carrot or a crisp cereal or stewed or bottled fruit, with a wheat germ or bran product and milk. Milk to drink or dandelion coffee.

Midday Conservatively cooked vegetables (potatoes always cooked or baked in their skins); or a raw salad; with egg dish or cheese dish or a vegetarian savoury of some kind.

Dessert: Fresh or stewed fruit or baked apple; or milk jelly or junket; or wholemeal pudding.

Evening Large mixed salad with dressing of olive oil and squeeze of lemon juice and grated cheese or milled nuts; with wholewheat bread or toast or crisp-bread and butter or margarine (and a yeast extract if wished).

Dessert: As for midday meal, or dried fruit, or piece of wholemeal cake, or glass of milk.

At night Fruit or vegetable drink or milky drink.

To conclude this chapter, I propose to deal with some important aspects of healthful dietetics which should be understood by the reader who wishes to set about arranging a completely vegetarian dietary for himself, if he is to obtain therefrom the maximum benefit to his health.

VITAMINS

Firstly, I shall deal with the question of *vitamins* (the special life-elements in food). This is a subject much to the fore these days, in any talk about diet, and it is as well for the vegetarian, or would-be vegetarian, to know which foods are rich in particular vitamins, so as to ensure an adequate intake of them in his dietary.

Actually, a diet planned along the lines indicated earlier in this chapter will contain a sufficiency of all vitamins as well as organic mineral salts, but it is just as well for the reader to have some more specific information on this important topic.

Vitamin A. This is a fat-soluble vitamin which is necessary for the health of the eyes, and for the health and protection of the respiratory tract, digestive function and the genito-urinary organs. This vitamin is found most richly in the following foods, in order of vitamin content: egg-yolk; milk; butter; cheese; green vegetables; carrots; tomatoes; dried fruits; fresh fruits; whole cereals.

Vitamin B^1. Vitamin B is a very complex, water-soluble vitamin which has been split up into many parts. In the present context, we need only be concerned with vitamins B^1 and B^2, as these are by far the most important of the group. Also, if these two B-vitamins are present in the diet, it is fairly certain that the rest of the

B-complex are present too.

Vitamin B^1 has been found to be one of the most important of all the vitaminic substances in the body, as its presence is essential if we are to metabolize our food properly.

No matter how much food we may consume, if sufficient intake of vitamin B^1 is not assured by our dietary, we shall not assimilate what we have eaten, as the metabolic processes of the body are depcndent upon an adequate supply of B^1 for all essential tasks. Thus, a deficiency in this vitamin can lead to malnutrition, digestive and bowel disorders, and more particularly to nerve disorders of all kinds, as the nerves are the first part of the bodily mechanism to be affected when the body is under-nourished, or when food is not being assimilated properly.

Vitamin B^1 is found in the following foods, in order of richness: yeast; yeast extracts; wheat-germ; wheat-germ products; bran; peanuts; dried peas, beans and lentils; nuts (except coconut); wholewheat; whole barley; rye; oatmeal; maize; natural brown rice; egg-yolk; fruits; vegetables.

Vitamin B^2 Complex. Under this heading are included vitamin B^7 (*nicotinic acid* or the *P.P. factor), lacto-* or *ribo-flavin,* and *adermin* (vitamin B^6). A deficiency of nicotinic acid in the diet is the cause of the deficiency disease *pellagra*, and there is no doubt that the whole B^2 complex is essential to the maintenance of health generally.

This vitamin is found in the following foods in order of abundance: dried yeast; yeast extracts; wheat-germ; wheat-germ products;

bran; wholewheat; whole-grain cereals generally.

Vitamin C. This vitamin is known as the *anti-scorbutic* vitamin, as its absence from the diet produces the disease known as *scurvy* (or *scorbutus*). This was a condition which used to affect seafaring men in the old days, forced to live for many months at a time on a diet entirely deficient in fresh vegetables or fruit. The inclusion of lime juice in their diet immediately stopped the ravages of the disease.

The most productive source of vitamin C is undoubtedly citrus fruits generally. An absence of this vitamin in the diet predisposes towards the development of pyorrhoea, to an unhealthy skin condition, and to lowered vitality generally.

The foods most productive of vitamin C, in order of value, are: black-currants; broccoli; cabbage (raw); turnip-greens; lemons; oranges; grape-fruit; limes; water-cress; red-currants; cauliflower (raw); swede turnips (raw); dried peas (sprouted two days); gooseberries; raspberries, loganberries; strawberries; pineapple; broad beans (raw); dandelion leaves; tomatoes; parsnips; leeks; potatoes (raw); bananas; apples; lettuce; beetroot (raw); cooked and canned fruits and vegetables.

Vitamin D. This is another fat-soluble vitamin like vitamin A, with which it is usually found closely associated. It is known as the *anti-rachitic* vitamin, as a deficiency of this vitamin produces the disease known as *rickets* (or *rachitis*). At the same time, it is now known that the body manufactures its own vitamin D when it receives a sufficiency of sunshine, and so the importance of the sun in relation to this vitamin is self-apparent. Children suffering from rickets have been cured by artificial sun-ray treatment (where frequent exposure to real sunshine was not practicable), as well as when given large doses of the actual vitamin.

Vitamin D is also essential for proper bone and teeth formation, and for the adequate utilization by the body of organic calcium. It is therefore a most important vitamin, and its chief vegetarian sources of supply, in order of value, are: egg-yolk; milk; butter; cheese; fresh fruits and vegetables (these latter in only very small quantities).

Vitamin D is therefore the one which vegans run most risk of not obtaining from their food, if they cut out all dairy products, but we must remember that the body manufactures its own supplies of this vitamin if there is sufficient sunshine available.

Vitamin E. This is known as the *fertility vitamin*, as its presence is said to be essential for proper conception and the production of children. This vitamin is found in most foods, and particularly in vegetable oils. It is very potent in wheat-germ and products made from this.

Other vitamins are constantly being discovered, as has been mentioned, but if the diet contains a sufficiency of the vitamins already referred to, it will undoubtedly contain all other vitamins too.

MINERAL-RICH FOODS

I now wish to say something about those foods that are richest in such mineral elements as iron, calcium and phosphorus. These are all vital elements in the development and maintenance of full health. Calcium and phosphorus are particularly essential for proper bone and tooth formation, whilst a sufficiency of iron in the blood is most important to prevent anaemia and oxygen-starvation (for it depends upon the available iron in the blood as to how much oxygen it can take up, at any one time, to distribute to the cells of the body).

Foods rich in *iron*, in order of value, are: lentils; egg-yolk; dried beans; black treacle; oatmeal; dried peas; wholewheat; dried currants; almonds; turnip-top greens; spinach; dates; raisins; eggs; olives; dandelion leaves; dried figs; prunes; chocolate; Scotch kale; green peas; asparagus; peanuts; broccoli; cheese.

Foods rich in *calcium*, in order of value, are: cheese; turnip-top greens; black treacle; almonds; Scotch kale; watercress; dried figs; egg-yolk; milk; broccoli; olives; dried beans; lentils; endive; spinach; chocolate; brown rice; currants; carrots; peanuts; oatmeal; turnips; celery; dandelion leaves; raisins; wholewheat; cabbage.

Foods rich in *phosphorus*, in order of value, are: cheese; egg-yolk; oatmeal; chocolate; almonds; cashew nuts; dried peas; dried beans; wholewheat; peanuts; lentils; walnuts; brown rice; dried currants; Brussels sprouts; raisins; milk; potatoes.

TRACE ELEMENTS

Other organic minerals needed by the body, in order to maintain its acid-alkaline balance, and essential for the upkeep of the organism generally, are: sodium, potassium, magnesium, silicon, sulphur, chlorine, manganese, iodine, fluorine, copper, etc.

Some of these elements are only required in minute traces, but if the diet is planned on the lines already indicated, and includes an abundance of fruit and vegetables and whole-grain products, these mineral requirements will be met easily. For iodine, seaweed and sea-plants are an extremely rich source, and *kelp* is a sea-plant product often used in conjunction with a reformed dietary because of its very rich mineral content (apart from its richness in organic iodine).

The calorific value of foods is something not stressed in reformed dietetics, as we do not subscribe to the orthodox view that energy comes from the food we eat. Our vital energy is derived from the source of life itself, and is not dependent on food intake, except that the food we eat is the means through which our vital energy expresses itself.

A vegetarian type of diet, along the lines here indicated, can ensure the fullest possible utilization of innate energy, because it allows maximum bodily efficiency and development of function.

Man does not live by bread alone, and when considering the question of a healthful diet we also have to bear in mind the need for maximum fresh air, exercise, sunshine, relaxation and sleep. All these various factors play their part in ensuring the body's fullest utilization of the food eaten, in their different ways, and it is most essential, therefore, for the reader to bear this fact always in mind.

RAW FOOD DIET

A subject of interest to many vegetarians and diet reformers is that of the *raw food diet.* Many people have found that food eaten raw retains its maximum health value, as it is then consumed in its most vital state, and there can be no doubt that the smaller the part played by cooked food in the diet, the better in every way, from the health point of view.

But those who are unused to such a dietary should exercise care in changing over to raw food, especially if they are getting on in years. It is best to begin with a daily menu as indicated in Chapter 7, and then, as one gets used to such a dietary, gradually cut out cooked food and substitute raw food. Those who wish to exclude bread may have raw wheat, or other wholegrains, ground and taken somewhat like porridge. In this case, however, an alternative source of dietary fat should be substituted for the butter or margarine which are usually eaten with bread.

CHAPTER 8

IN CONCLUSION

I have purposely kept this book as short as possible, yet it contains the most salient facts and arguments relative to vegetarianism generally. In it I may have said a few hard things about vegetarians themselves, but only in order to make some of the more hidebound and orthodox-minded of them realize that by their acts and opinions they are holding up the spread of the movement they hold so dear.

There is an enormous scope for the development of vegetarianism in this country, not to speak of the rest of the world, and it should be the object of every vegetarian to aid this development by example as well as by word of mouth. There is surely nothing more convincing to non-vegetarians than to meet vegetarians who both look and are *healthy* in the highest degree?

Pale and hollow-cheeked vegetarians do nothing but a disservice to vegetarianism by their appearance, despite the fact that there are millions of non-vegetarians who look as bad if not worse than they do, physically. But the public at large do not view the matter from that angle. A vegetarian to them is someone *on trial*; he is on perpetual trial for his views and opinions and way of life. He can only come through the ordeal successfully by showing conclusively *in himself* that the vegetarian mode of living gives far more in return to those adopting it than does the conventional meat-eating one.

It is hoped, therefore, that this book will help many vegetarians to adjust their ideas and ways of thinking generally to the needs of the situation, and so enable them to 'put their vegetarian house in order.' In the case of many of them it needs doing so badly, I fear, from what I know of the way many of them eat and live.

I must stress again that *it is not sufficient* just to leave flesh foods out of one's dietary and trust to luck that everything will be all right. One must tackle the question *intelligently*, and this can only be done successfully by combining vegetarian principles with scientific *diet reform.* Only then can vegetarianism vindicate itself fully in the public eye, and demonstrate that through it lies the way to full health of mind and body.

It is not enough to embrace vegetarianism as an ideal, as many do; it must be adopted as a way of life *superior to the conventional one*! It is essentially from that angle that I have tackled the subject in this book, and I hope its fruits will amply justify my labours!

In conclusion, I should like to say a few words about those little-thought-of people *behind* the vegetarian movement: those firms who make the health foods sold at Health Food Stores. They deserve a special word of praise from all vegetarians, for it is safe to say we could not get on without them. May their good services for the movement continue for many decades!

Finally, I should like to thank Mr Roy Walker, the former Secretary of the London Vegetarian Society, for his kindness in loaning me some material for the writing of this book. His ready assistance in this matter is much appreciated, and I sincerely hope that through the book the membership of the society will be appreciably swelled in due course.